I love that you're my

Brother

because

I Love You Because Books
www.riverbreezepress.com

To my Brother

From:

_____

Date:

_____

The best thing about you is your

_____

I am amazed at your talent for

_____

You are better than

_____

You should win the
grand prize for

_____

You make me feel special when

_____

We would make a great

_____

team

I love when you tell me about

_____

I love when we

_____

together

You taught me how to

_____

I remember when we

_____

I wish I could

---

as well as
you do

I love that we have the same

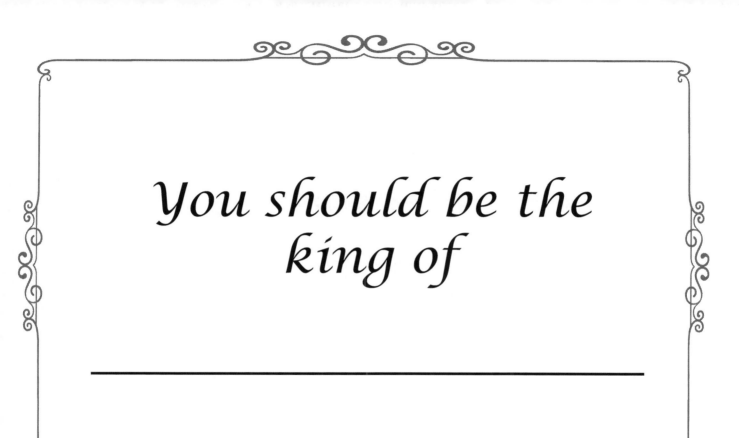

You should be the king of

_____

If you were a superhero you would be

_____

You make me laugh
when you

_____

I wish I had more time to

_____

with you

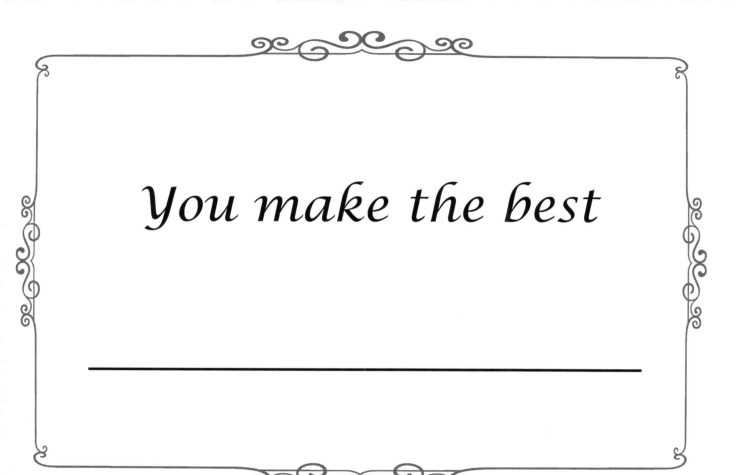

You make the best

_____

You have
inspired me to

_____

If I could give you anything it would be

_____

I would love to go

_____

with you

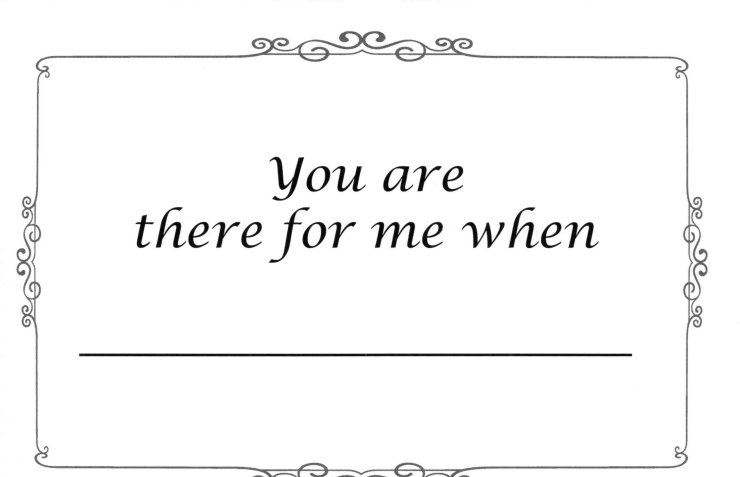

You are
there for me when

_____

*I love you
because you are*

_____